# Dreams And Dirges

Melanie McCurdie

Copyright © 2016 Melanie McCurdie
All rights reserved.
ISBN-13: 978-0-9951525-8-8

For Nana
1922-201

# ACKNOWLEDGMENTS

We all have people who influence us in different ways, some simply by being there. Those individuals make life sweet as pie.

As always, for Muse. Without his sparkly ass, and never-ending shenanigans, I would be lost.

Foggy McCorrigan, for the friendship, encouragement and always honest responses that I know I can count. Thank you so much.

Patti Beeton, Carolyn Graham, Thomas Davis, Amy Kling, Kelly Brandsness, and Rachel Kent-Harris; each one of you brings a special kind of light to my day. Even if it's simply a *meerkat* in my direction, it means the world to me. XO

## *Mine*

Yes,
once I compared you a summer's day
Then you were winsome and light
Now the darkness has stolen that
And replaced it with a different lust
For life
For death
You are my raison d'être

## *Be-*

Lain Beneath
Once Believed
Veracity suspect, bewildered
Every word leaves me bemused
Should love bedazzle your eyes
It behooved one to be wary
Lest you find yourself besotted
Beguiled by your own yearning
And left benighted, alone

## *Run, Reaper*

I despise Reaper, currently
That motherfucker is off
Polishing his bone or playing
Peeping Grim through some portal
The perv.
Hey!! Bonedaddy!
Think you could stop rubbing one out
And do your damned job?
For once? Instead of dicking about

MELANIE MCCURDIE

## *Dirge*

Don't be too kind to me
I'm only human and like it or not
There's still a heart ticking away in here.
Worse yet, it feels things and I'm tired.
Stupid thing,
it still wants to believe that maybe,
words aren't all doggerel and dirges
secrets and lies and wooful design.
so, please, don't be too kind
I may believe you.

## *Mothersuckers*

Hickory duckory
Fuck, why must you be such a dick?
If buzzkill had a finger,
it'd be pointed in your general vicinity
Is it so difficult to be
a little less self-aware, maybe?
Screw your thinly veiled, venomous barbs
I'm hanging out in drown town tonight
Let my sorrows sink or whatever
I'll smother the mothersuckers.
Or if I must, I'll hotbox the cabin
Leave 'em breathless and
watch them fly away

MELANIE MCCURDIE

## *Reboot Juice*

Another-day/
Wake-and-die/
Suffocation-again/sigh/
It's-not-ideal-perhaps/
But-I-embrace-it/why-not/
Life-is-so-much-simpler/
-when-you're-dead/
Shit-doesn't-matter-except-the-day/
And-the-people-in-it/
Cursed-daystar/hiss/
Death-goes-on-into perpetuity/
Mournings-suck-even for-the-departed/
That's-why-there's-coffee.

## *Chary*

You remind me of someone.
Something says be wary;
It's the manner that you carry,
the method of speech, rings bells
of the warning variety...
Stupidly, as the reasoning is not sound.
There is no cause for distrust –
Fear can cause brain cells to self-destruct –
no reason but this terminal case
of silly suspicion
I've been blessed with and yet
it niggles at my memory banks ...
You remind me of someone.

MELANIE MCCURDIE

## *Thirsty Work*

I want a drink.
It is thirsty work
Fighting your daemons
Why not just give in?
The bottle beckons;
Dance, the cruel tease she
Makes the poison glow
The potion relieves
Just one sip will make
It all better – but
It won't nor can it.
Just another lie
Like that from your lips

## *Expression*

My lips yearn for a soulful kiss
Fresh as mown grass that tastes as sweet
Your strength comes as the night settles
It falls as I do time and time again
To my knees, dusk surrounds us
I want you to show me the
darkness in your grasp
As I withdraw into the shadows
Would you take my hand?
Let me not fade back to my comfort
but lead me forward, into the trees
into the meadows, to run
To Feed and feast, to lay and love
and fade in the rising sun

MELANIE MCCURDIE

## *Stains*

Punches leave stains.
people call them bruises but
stains is more accurate.
words leave stains, too.
they hunch shoulders and
they burn in your chest, and
they mar your view of yourself
until all you see is ugly.
they scar your body in ways
that no one else can see.
some stains can be removed
given enough time, trust and soul bleach,
but the truth of it is that
some stains never fade.

## *illogical study*

You are illogical

The way that things are/
Nothing in your mind/
Nothing makes sense/
in comparison to/
the human condition/
no rhymes and no reason/
I do not understand/
How you can be so –
Save a libidinal overcompensation

## *4 ...3 ... 1 fin*

I'm unhappy.
Deeply so, and there's not a damned thing
to do,  that can be done to ease the ache,
rather, the sting.

go ahead - shake your head - it's quite fine.
Understand, though, that life can be a
royal twat and her choice of torture
for your punishments or transgressions
is very much different from mine.

decisions, they rarely involve just
the one who is making them.

okay?

Fin

## DREAMS AND DIRGES

## *The Throes*

Your kiss is pain,
a blinding pressure that tears me apart
Your hand close to my breast, searing –
how it burns as my teeth
find your lips and sink deeply
They bleed, filling my mouth with salty warmth
I twist in your embrace with your hand
at my back pulling me closer,
hard against your delight
and it's excruciating, exquisite agony
The final throes
Oh, I die in your arms, body trembling,
Aquiver and die, again

## *It never ends*

I wish I had the ferocious wordocity to explain how it is and how it feels. I'm unable describe the rabid veracity of the sound and taste of that voice that runs around in my head. I wish that I had a way to convey to you the vibrating baritone shivers or the mid-tone chill in my bones. How it cycles like rats on a squeaky wheel, the way it drives me batshit with frustration to make it stop.

It never ends. Over and over, the monstrously melodic notes forever repeat like the definition of crazy, except eventually crazy stops if you stab it enough times. So, I could go with the flow and just let it take me. After all, it doesn't define me if I drop off the edge because that voice is driving me insane. Motherfucker keeps singing it never ends.

I've become a master at hiding the pain behind a smile so that nobody knows how much I want it all to end.

DREAMS AND DIRGES

## *Crackles*

Ye feculent maggots
Such slithering horrors come to
Roil on the putrid shores
Where the polka-dotted crackles fly
Why, Hell is salty as lonely tears
This sandy reclamation serves no purpose
But to be agreeably macabre
Maid, she laughs, in chilling madness
Like a million bootfalls in unison
And it stings with flares on full alert
Inhale water and breathe fire,
She sings, and snickers
Knowing that it's an egregious error
To giggle at death, unless you're his girl

MELANIE MCCURDIE

## *Perspective*

He says I'm beautiful, but
I think his eyes are malfunctioning.
Nothing in the mirror shows
anything close to that description.
What I see are lines and scars,
cracked crystal memories;
Things I do not wish to remember,
are what I face every day.
Someone suggested, implied,
that my soul was leaking through the veil
and I cried until I laughed
at the deadly sweet naivety.
The undead don't have a soul.
Look in the glass, the empty vessel
mourns the perspective he sees.

## *But you love me, right?*

I talk, for once, about my feelings
and you get angry, or tune me out
Or just flat out ignore
But hey, you love me, right?

I can sit for hours and listen to
This and that about who and what
About everything under the sun
Until I start to discuss matters of
Importance.
Somehow the conversation gets derailed
*Back to you.*
But hey, you love me, right?

I'm struggling. Badly.
So much on my mind that I'm lost
And I have nowhere to turn.
There's no one around that doesn't
Appear to view me as a tool.
But hey, you love me, right?

MELANIE MCCURDIE

## *Prince of Stones*

Promised me you'd stick
like glue, true blue, to the end
but you split like a coward
are you so empowered,
that you break word like bread,
it's easy to blame, play the game
like a player, roll the dice,
you always win, such a sin
but honey, players get played
your excuses are staid and
worth little more than nothing
superman you ain't but darlin,
to remove the sting
always remember,
a pauper can be king
if he plays the real game
a word to the wise,
I'll cut it down to manageable size
just end the bullshit riddles
and speak your mind.

## *Sleepless*

I'm tired, and battle-sore
I'm awake and alone, and the world so quiet
Its too dark and
I'd sell my soul to be able to rest
To not see the terrible things
my mind shows me
Too scared to close my eyes
and helpless to fight it
I can't sleep, not for days and days
Not since that night on the rooftop
Not since then and I see you everywhere
In the shadowy corners and sinister doorways
Since then,
You are haunt my days and steal my nights
Slowly driving me out of my head

MELANIE MCCURDIE

## *The words*

They say that hindsight is 20/20.
It certainly lends a certain clarity;
Realisation through recollection
The words
were
(are)
just that
(words)
Full of sentiment and
(but)
signifying nothing
I think that what hurts the most
is the knowledge that not once,
while whining your woes,
Did you think to ask about me.

## *The Eyeroll Game*

Who left the bag of idiots open?
Who is going to take care of the infestation?
*Snickering wildly*
An idiot infestation
I'm surrounded by them
And there are no inoculations

It could just be my magnetic personality or
I'm the eye of the fucking storm
*tornado noises*
Perhaps I've accomplished
What took losing a body to succeed in doing
Don't be daft. I haven't killed anyone...yet
I'm taking gravitational pull here

Maybe it's something in the air or
Poison in the water or *squee*
The zombie apocalypse, at long last

One thing is for damned sure
If things are going to shit
At least it will be quiet for a change

## *Ties*

Do you have any idea how damaging
this situation is?
Restrained and escape is improbable
any time soon.
Fighting the urge to cry is as exhausting,
if not more
Than fighting my Daemon's insistence that

WE
MUST BE
FREE OF
THIS MONSTROSITY

WE
MUST NOT
BE
CONTAINED

It's like battling your brain's knowledge
of fact with a deep- seated desperation
to deny, dismember, depart
It's upsetting enough,
when there's no other choice –
I'm just no good at this stuff
But I'm trying…

## *Photograph*

I don't know you,
But you fascinate me
I think as I watch,
how you slither and slink
An Ermine in spring
Ingeniously wrapping your fingers
And squeezing, flattening my lungs
with the weight of your stare,
stealing my air

Not a word spoken, just a photo
That holds my attention,
words written, smitten,
but I don't know you
I'm drawn to your madness,
that capers unbidden,
uncontrolled in your features
I wish to tear out your eyes and
replace my own
So that I may see what you do,
as you do

Because you fascinate me

MELANIE MCCURDIE

# After the Storm

stay calm

*(that's just stupid)*

**can't breathe**

*(duh dumbass i tried to warn you)*

drumbeats in my ears are too loud

(nah that's just your heart about to explode)
(fun innit?)

in terror and I'm alone

why are my eyes wet?

*(you cry?)*
*(holy shit.)*
*(i thought you were made of stone)*
*(...lungs burn yet?)*

**they hurt**

*(now you know how I feel)*

## DREAMS AND DIRGES

where is the air?

*(no air for you!!)*
*(you're not going to die, you know)*

oh hell and eternal damnation
 the brittle failings,
they hang like raindrops on needles

*(kinda like teardrops on lashes)*

They aren't much different after the storm

## The Ticking

Tick-tock

                                           pacepacepacepacepace

Tick-tock

                                        Has the clock stopped?

Tick-tock

                 Seriously? Not even a minute yet?

Tick

                                      Time is just a myth ...

Tock

                Fuck

Time, in our limited perception, only exists in our minds....so the so-called experts say. Whoever THEY are...

However, when a body is positioned, poised and waiting, it becomes torture to the impatient, the desperate...This non-existent perception of time seems pretty damned real...I wonder if the ticking of the clock is the sound of Reaper's heart

## *Statue of She*

She sits in silence, her eyes closed with a sweet distracted smile on her lips, trying to blend in with the crowd and fails. She wasn't meant to blend in. Instead, she stands out like a glorious statue in the middle of a war-torn slum and is blissfully unaware of the watchful stares.

At the mention of her name, those sapphire lasers flicker open in shock and dismay; in anger at being exposed and she bores holes into the one who drew the unwanted attention. With uncomprehending tears, she feels betrayed, embarrassed and looks away with a sigh and a flush of her cheeks. And closes her pretty eyes again as though her actions were an invisibility cloak.

She can never see that she is beautiful, that insecure creature with a masque glued firmly in place. She doesn't understand that when the masque lifts, that she shines like the devil dressed in Angel's wings.

MELANIE MCCURDIE

## *Tequila and Tears*

Someone
told me
that
happiness
will never
be found
at the
bottom
of any
bottle,
that only
numbness and
tears lived there
and I believed him
until I discovered
that numbness has
its merits and that
tequila and tears
make a fine mixture
in which to drown in

DREAMS AND DIRGES

## *Soul Synapsis*

Yeah I hear you moaning
In your Emojish tongues
It's all in the vernacular

Don't you know?

There is no cure for acerbic wit

It's hardly a sickness
Twitch the bitch switch, I'm down if it is

Today, the social diction is
hardly spectacular
Sadly lacking the eloquent factor
I miss the pretty words

I find, too, that my vascular capacity
is next to null
I think I have a slow leak
Maybe I'm a Synapsid out of its prime
A soul Synapsis

I still love you though
In my eyes, everything is irie
We stay gold, just like Pony Boy
Like the last whit of light in the sky

## *Marley*

There she sits, this Goddess
in a Marley t-shirt and plain black panties
The way the shirt is plastered
to her small frame,
it accentuates those perfect breasts
the chill in the room as plain as the
nipples poking through the thin fabric

Supple, slim, my hands itch to touch
The smooth porcelain of her flesh
and feel her long legs quiver under the
Flats of my palms while they travel down,
then between
All that is nonexistent in the regard
To the eyes that stare holes in my soul
This Goddess creature dressed
in commoner's skin
I forget that she shuns the comparison
Beauty believes she is the beast

## *Cracklin'*

The sounds of silence.

There is no such thing
In reality.
Why? You are human.
Noise comes naturally
Y'know that crack'lin?
That rapid rushing
When hear something
And you are alone?

That's the cry of your nervous system

How about that thud
That beats in your ears...
Can't you hear it now?
Boom (pause) Boom (pause) (pause)
BOOM and your heart screams

That's the song of your heart pumping blood
through your veins

Silence is a misnomer for sound

MELANIE MCCURDIE

## *Which Tale*

Once upon a time,
The tale begins, as all fairy stories do,
When we all loved in the forest
And everybody loved everyone else
Except,

Once upon a time,
The memories were sweet
As apple blossoms on the morning
Like spun sugar on a hot summer day
It was all perfect, but

Once upon a time.
The flare of passion burned as relentlessly
As the fires under a cauldron and
twice as hot and then,

Once upon a time stopped being a fairy story
And became a scary tale...
Well fuck that noise.
I'll make my own story thanks

## *Agony, Ecstasy*

There, in the shadows, in the night. I see you. Strange as it seems, I know you Even as you advance, stalk, prey, I pray to some god; a Classic Deity for protection and hitch in a breath to scream

My dream, you tear me away, destroy me; your teeth gain entry as does your blood engulfed lust. O desirous disastrous syncopation, my heart sings decimation with climactic tones, first in pleasure, then in pain. In a greater ecstasy, hearts pound harder. All I see are your eyes, green-grey, glowing.

Blood red roses fall from your lips, salty and warm, ignites a thirst I cannot quench in droplets. You refuse me your kisses while you take pleasure in my body. A dying scream, a whispered moan, my mouth filled with death and flowers.

Peace at last

## *Wet Stone*

These are the truth tools;
these which I use to torture myself.
The sharpening stone must be wet and
the tools sharp to hit home.

I think I'm insane,
or at the least,
not so far from that ledgefall
into hell or beyond.
Thanks be Gods.

No emotion,
but that needling hot nothingness
and a bucketload of tears and fears
with nowhere to direct them.

I have nothing to say because –

I have no control.

Nothing will change the inevitable.
I cannot change the inevitable.
I have no control over the inevitable.

And I fucking hate it.

## *New Bones*

Someone asked me what I feel,
And to my own fault I responded
The only way that I know how.
Only Haywire live wire seemed apt.
It makes no sense, perhaps,
To anyone but me
But that's what it feels like.
It's as though my bones have been replaced
And the new ones simply vibrate
Until my teeth rattle.
It's oppressive and I'm trapped
By unseen eyes that observe
Every step, every breath
Someone is always there and it's no comfort
Nor replacement for flesh and blood.
It's uneasy the way the world is imploding
and the people are discussing politics
Issues of no consequence.
Leaves me to wonder what happens
What to those of us awake
When it ends.

MELANIE MCCURDIE

## *Storm*

It's something like a tornado
the way the universe tends to
turn. what's a girl to do, one thinks?
as she sprays her life with gasoline
and lights a match just to watch
it's birth; once, twice, thrice and again.
she does nothing more than giggle,
make popcorn and watch the world burn.

"clear skies ahead in the eyes
of the dead," she sighs wiping
tears from her cheeks and i relate
because i know the struggle to
keep breathing. the creature creeping;

it's not real, but it is. i don't
comprehend how it is that they
cannot see the storm building, or
hear the thunders roar.  it never
stops to stupefy, boggle the
mind; bleating sleeping sheep in fear
afraid of a silly spirit.

watch the way they mill about
frantic when the winds begin to
whip chaos into a frenzy.
pray to the almighty absent
for sanctuary if it helps
i can't grasp the concept of it
i don't understand the way you prey.

## *Son of a –*

Tiptoe through ground glass but leave no bloody footprints behind. Confuzzled by the contradictory message? Welcome to my world. I suggest you run.

You're still here? interesting. my thoughts about the situation go as thus: Winter's Chill is a twat. On it's heels, the Agoniser comes with his pretty, pain poisoned stick this son of a skunkbutt...his main pleasure in existence is to torture and torment everyone.

As you see, what goes on upstairs, isn't pretty. those damned squatters have set up shop in the braincase are back and they have drawn some fairly apt, if pornographically accurate, representations of reality.

And now, to the chagrin of only me, there's a high frequency vibration that has settled into my bones. an epically proportional ache that is slowly driving me utterly bonkers with a touch of batshit.

Sound fun?

## *Frisson*

Tired and woozy from lack of sleep, the bottles of wine numbing my senses and I stagger to bed, drunk and regretting, fall to the pillows and wishing upon wishes that I find myself somewhere *\*yawn\** other than *here* again and here is so good, so good and so right. I never could have imagined such a warmth, nearly molten, and feels like forever in Hell.

I like it so much – I can hear it calling me to drink and I do, swilling it around in my mouth, feel it coating my teeth. It tastes spicy, like cider, in winter and I can't get enough but you stop ticking and your blood flows sluggishly. The frisson that trembles my bones makes me drop you lifeless or nearly, to the ground. In horror, I hear your heart beating; it scares me, excites me, and time moves like your lips, seductive as you whisper, spraying droplets, *"please,"* and I wake, laughing.

MELANIE MCCURDIE

## *Keyholes*

Sometimes I swear I sense you,
Around corners in the hallways
Peeking from keyholes in forbidden rooms
That pisses me off.
In those moments, I hate you for leaving me.

In those moments, I hate you
and that's when I feel you
Standing too close and snickering
I turn, half hoping to see your snarky grin
Or just the warmth of your arms

Even as I open my eyes,
I know that it's a dream. A wish.
Never a day goes by that I don't think about
how you are the lucky one.

You don't have to remember
I don't want to forget

## *Some World ...*

It's the Opiate of the masses.

Opinion seems to act as some sort of aphrodisiac, and media? Media provides the soundtrack to the insanity.

It all makes us believe that if we kiss the ring on the hand of some pauper prince - if we commit ourselves to the real daemon by believing in the falsehoodery - that somehow everything will be status quo.

It's heresy; Your grass marriage with reality is really just a nest of lies brought to you solely by your inability to look past the mask into the windowless soup of Society's heart.

It's disheartening to feel alone in a world full of people, knowing that the black sheep is really just a warrior with a psychic advantage.

And that those with open minds remain the only armour that stands between the intentionally ignorant and those willing to see

## *Erect Thorn, Bare Windows*

Fearsome.
You are fearsome, lady,
from those eyes that hide some kind of
beautiful brain that coincides perfectly
with the savage monster you hide inside
oh I pretend that I don't notice
or care but I do and I want to not be
like all the others but baby,
you're killing me here
It isn't just my blood pressure that rises
whenever you walk by, ai,
I can't help but stare,
Gods...that derrière,
Yeah stop looking at me like I'm
some kind of prédateur, mon amour,
You have no worry from me, you see,
All this is secret, trapped in my mind,
Because I can barely breathe
when you're near
Let alone speak, or meet your eyes
other than the occasional glance in
The mirrored reflection, it's distracting

God, I wish I could say hello.

## *Snarligators*

The pterosaurs glide, hither and yon
On the hunt for the not quite dead
We call them Freshies.
Like a treat

Below the snarligators sunbathe
Hoping for a snack of their own
Poor things.

Here I sit in my library,
staring at walls instead of reading
In my laboratory bodies rot, waiting...

I'm no princess.
I don't need saving
Sometimes I play at being a Queen
The Fool giggles too hard at that joke –

Somewhere in the Minotaur's labyrinth
Lost inside some ancient catacomb
There is another freak, wandering
Looking for another heartless monster,
just like me

MELANIE MCCURDIE

*sigh* I'm distracted.
It's my world. I made it, flaws and all
Sleep is a fleeting friend, that twat
I'd give anything to engage in
A search for the soulless tonight

## Ragged Sails

Some say it's an invidious action, to place oneself in such a precarious position. Dancing with a better class of Daemon is the summative response to life on a ledge. Ah, but Evil speaks in such romantic rhetoric; pretty, lilting half-truths pleading to be believed.

One is always struggling with that temptation; refuting the historical evidence as naught, when even the intricacy of Hell's hegemony wanes from time to time.

Watch them frolic in the bête noire like children splashing in a sun shower.

I prefer the manner of Pale Death. Reaper speaks simply, the language of Souls, and his way is a recrudescence of full truth. Lanterns of fact in a world of lies.

One supposes that it is the best way. Biting back with kindness is similar to good deeds against a better class of Devils. Sort of like letting them starving to life during a harvest of fools.

MELANIE MCCURDIE

## *Broken Gate*

what? who me? ...
You can see me?

Thank You for asking –
i know that it's just a thing people say

it ain't pretty – run...
why're you still here?
*sigh* fine. You asked ...

there are bleaker days, storms ahead and
i'm already tired -feeling small
all hands on deck
it's going to be a bumpy landing

jebus i hate it enough when I fly
in some magical avionic nightmare
Terra Firma should be more stable –
yet here i am, back on the ground
Hurray!!! skinned knees!!
i'm wondering if- why should i –
i just don't want to get back up

## DREAMS AND DIRGES

don't feel like breathing anymore
barely am anyway, these days
more like sucking a Pete's Drive-In shake
through a cocktail straw
and it's far more effort than it's worth

still, it's better than the alternative
i hear the transition is a bitch

MELANIE MCCURDIE

# *A Bird's Eye View*

*ruffles feathers*
its cold out here
on this stupid
branch in this tree
Freezing, watching
the weeping old
man, sitting in
his saggy old
chair by the big
bay window yank
his only thin
brown blanket tight
around his frail
shoulders and shake
*blink and shudder*
without feathers
i would freeze too
but he has a
home to go with
that brown blanket
while i freeze here
on this stupid
branch in this tree

## *Maybe*

    I despise the word desperate, yet the scrabbly, bitey thoughts, the ones that rattle like rats in a rucksack offer no other bon mot in place

    Unfortunately, desperation aside, I'm afraid and dumbstruck, the daemon stole my tongue – so easily stolen – but …

  must you make me twitch, ye perpetual devil?
  ~ I'm trying to be serious so listen!

    *ajuster ma couronne*

    You've been like glue and I love you for it. What's more, I'm astonished…undeserving.

    For Sanity's Sake, would you please stop grinning you mean old thing! Playing peekaboo on the mirror's edge… I still win.

    You're not getting a medal, you know, for your torturous truth bombs … Perhaps, on further consideration, a Purple Heart for braving teeth and tears, unflinchingly. Without judgement…maybe

## *Plagued by a Promise*

I remember the racket.
That noisy daemon behind the smile.
How could I forget?

Some say I fell in love with you that day
and maybe they're right. Love as a brother,
the first truthsayer in my life.
My friend.

What resonates strongest, and most often
are those quiet sober moments that weren't
laugher and gaiety, but factual and
less than tactful.

The words, though, they still stick.
"My dear, you'll die. Will you die on
your terms or conditions of someone else?"

The answer was then, on my terms.
The answer today remains the same.

## DREAMS AND DIRGES

I'd be lying to say there aren't still days
when I sit down to text you about
some stupidity or a problem that only your
unedited POV can illuminate and
I get halfway through, before I remember
that it's useless, that it's a message
you'll never get.

I hate that, but I promised,
you motherfucker. so, you win again.

## *Mind Junk*

I don't want to sleep yet.

Funny,
I'd forgotten all those sweet sleepy sounds
That come after smiles and laughs and –
and –

*sigh*

I'm forcibly reminded tonight about how
life is fleeting and it's damned difficult to
accept the concept of just how fast
things change.

Time travel isn't impossible?

Are you sure?

Just blink and a decade is gone.  Two.
How fast things change …
I just don't want to miss a second when time
keeps slipping through my fingers.
It's already half passed and
I don't want it to be.

I hate it

Sometimes there are no choices,
Just that helpless feeling that there's
nothing to be done but worry
and wonder and wait.

I just – It's that – I don't want to sleep yet.

# Flash

I remember all too well. that agonizing thread of fear, the disbelief and then the anvil that takes out your will, your ability to stay sane.

Steals your breath, it does, it steals your mind, giggling silver bells and then – then, everything stops.

Your heart freezes, it catches and beats, then stutters again, pounding heavily in your ears, and you wonder why?

WHY?!
JESUS FUCKING CHRIST WHY?

Then you begin to torture yourself with the constant replay, the what ifs and the maybes, just to be sure there wasn't one action, one word, anything that could've changed the outcome.

The helplessness. It threatens to turn you weak sister, and despite the brutal pep-talk, the only you can do is sit and shatter.

I understand the rage at not being able to change a thing, at the inability go back and do something that could affect the outcome.

Desperate to wake up from the horror.
But no, it's all real, every horrid moment of this nightmare is not a dream but an alternate reality.

Real. Final, forever and you think. With a sigh, why - Just...why?

I remember. I understand

MELANIE MCCURDIE

## *Love you more*

I didn't know what to say
I never meant for her to feel that way
But it killed me to hear her cry
from behind the bathroom door
You don't love me anymore

Your smile never touches your eyes
The one on your face I barely recognize
Losing you cuts to the core
Because I know you don't love me anymore

She can't see me standing here
Listening to her tears
Hurting from the fear
When she sighs, then softly cries
You don't love me anymore

I could just run away
Something always makes me stay
There is no one else to look for
You are the one
So how can you say I don't love you anymore

You think I don't care
You can't see it so it's not there
Blind lady love

# DREAMS AND DIRGES

You are what my heart cries for
Truly, I couldn't love you more

She can't see me standing here
  Cheeks wet from my tears
  Hurting when she sighs

You don't love me anymore
I really couldn't love you more

## *The Hangin' Tree*

I knew we were forever on that late January night when you carved our initials in the stained bark, in that dark at the base of the Hangin' Tree, sealing a pact, a promise that I gave freely, you came to me, dressed in the flesh of one I adored, an almost man, and I surrendered my soul, the gift of my virginity. Under the full moon, I surrendered time and time again, made yours, my blood. Yours. I tasted your years in each mouthful while you fed me, bled for me, made me yours and promised you'd never go.

That was before. This is now. Here I find myself again, here under the Hangin' Tree, decades have passed since you made your vow.

Now, after having fed from the small town, a delicious virginal boy with the scruff of a beard dirtying his cheeks crept from the shadows. I let him take me. Let him spend his youthful exuberance with his hands tearing at the expensive fabric of my dress, and fumbling at my breasts with inexperienced glee. Let him fill me with his loathsome seed.

He smelled like my garden. A riot of fragrances that lingers still wafting up my nose when he fell back, his face smeary with pleasure. I took his life. The savory taste of his fearful lust is so intoxicating. See how he lays there?

How he resembles the fragile creatures with bodies frail as the winter dawn? An innocent cherub waiting for a paradise that will never be his. His is a face that will be the ruin of many hearts and existences. The Angel awakes; Death comes.

MELANIE MCCURDIE

## *Blind Man's Bluff*

Should our eyes ever meet
across a crowded room or in close proximity,
You know that I could never hide my heart

It's a fact: I'm poor poker player.
My cards I hold in my eyes
as much as on my sleeve
And I'm afraid to want,
scared to feel,
I don't want to be one of those
gushy mushy women
Naive and laughable

A joke.

My love isn't given freely and
for a few that hold me close,
it is real and it is true

Not in a pretty box but torn and bleeding.

Love isn't a sparkling jewel…
it is body and mind,
messy and beautiful.

I own nothing more precious to give

## *Caustic*

    I once compared you to a summer's day. You are a sweet dream, one that wakes me in a sheen of sweat with your name on my lips. Pretty – but with a personality much more caustic, more akin to steel wool covered in flowers and pretty words. A noxious festering seed of hate that you carry like a Prada bag, leaving me to wonder about the state of my mind.

    Your pain is my pleasure, when your smile turns to a grimace as I flay alive you with my tongue. More arousing is the fear that fills your light eyes, turning them brighter as you fight for your life and I squeeze you tight to my chest, my lips on yours.

    Your breath, your body, your mind -

    Please never stop

## *Cologne*

It's getting late, the moon high in the sky. So am I, but not so much that I don't - *I don't* - feel his weight on the bed, so familiar that I can time my breathing by the soft exhale when he lies down behind me. The scent of that horrible cologne that I would endlessly tease him about dizzying but not so much that I can pretend not to feel the light touch of his fingers; lips on the nape of my neck, making me shiver and through the window, the moon moves higher.

I roll to my right, hair spread like a silky blanket on the pillow, becoming damp with my tears. My breath is stolen, frozen and flushed because. He is here, and this is the last good day, the last time before the drugs that ate his body took hold of his mind.

This is how I remember him. This Moment, belly to belly, after love with the windows open listening to the crickets saw house serenade. His eyes. Smile. Like this. Like now. *But it can't be real.* I close my eyes, afraid to open them, praying that I'm wrong.

Praying I'm right.  I can't feel him anymore; he's gone from me again but I still smell that godawful cologne and my skin still shivers. I grieve again, grateful and devastated

## *Cracked*

I love you too. You are mine in ways
that you will never
belong to another,
In places, you are imbedded in my flesh
And that will never change.

What has changed, is my heart.
I just can't keep suffering cracks and
Tiny fissures that Gorilla glue won't fix.
The center can't hold.
It doesn't mean I'm lost or gone.
I'm hardly invisible.
It just means that starting today,
I love me more than anyone else.

I've never let me down,
Always stood true and loyal
No matter the war that raged around me,
Only detaching myself when
I was feeling those last few
grasping heartbeats of dying love.

Then, it was kinder to just inflict the wound,
viciously if necessary, to cut attachments.
It's the only way I can still see you,
and not long for what was.

# DREAMS AND DIRGES

Sometimes, you have to choose between
bleeding out or tying on a tourniquet.

I've bled; lost my way, made mistakes,
found love and destroyed that too.

I love you.

I could repeat it over and over
But I see from your expression
That you will never believe it.
I know it doesn't take the sting away,
And it convinces neither of us.

Although I do.

Does your chest hurt?
Does it burn?
I'm sorry it must be this way.
It hurts me too,
like a knife slowly twisting alive
between my ribs.

Like the one twisting between yours.

A painful last kiss
Hot are the flames that burn for you,
hot as your blood coating my fingers.
*I love you*, I whisper. *but I love me more*

## *Leave you to Bleed*

You might think I hate you and make no mistake, **I do**; the very air that you breathe is an offence to my existence. It makes my head scream.

My fists are pounding against the brick wall that is my forehead, beating back the impulses that drive me to blank rage. Percussive, concussive - all day it bangs and throbs, and my conscience is tired.

Delirious, and exhausted, it settles, still standing, eyes closed against the wall and whispers lacklustre defences; the constant refrain of silently wishing I'd take the initiative and ram this meat fork into your balls, twist and tear until you can't scream any longer.

I could have watched you jitter and dance to the rhythm of the falling blood. Leave you to bleed out on the floor with my spit drying in your eyes and smiling as your life ebbs away slowly and painfully, crying your woes to your non-existent

God. Oh, to laugh and titter, to tell you the truth. *There is no God and you are in Hell.* You die with denials on your lips...

MELANIE MCCURDIE

## *Reflection*

He sits, head cocked,
Breath deepening, listening, nodding.

Do you hear me or like the firelight?
Am I only reflection?
She softly asks, wary.
Curiously, quietly sighs.

Pen in hand
Black ink tracing
Soothing the growl
Snarling smiling lips
Pretty words yearning
Tiny irritating scratches

I hear you
He mutters, low
Not a reflection
Please don't go
And she startles
Beginning to fade

Then, he lifts his eyes
The pen like a lighthouse
It coaxes, draws her nearer

Closer she creeps, a shadow
Wraith in the flamboyant light
His hand moving gently, deliberately
Not unnoticed, a darkness dancing.
As above, as below
He stands before her
His stare ruinous desire
Breath quickens, stroking, invoking

His hand
Her cheek
His mouth
Her lips

He is
She is
They are
Real

MELANIE MCCURDIE

## *The Dwindling Dream*

You keep asking me as though
whatever crap falls from my lips
is some kind of gospel
or carries weight,
but it is worth less then nothing.


I'd laugh but it's just so damned sad
when people trust the word of a ghost


Why do you care what I think?
Why, exactly, does it matter?


There's not a god damned thing
going on upstairs;
empty noggins only breed cobwebs,
those things are hardly substantial
enough to catch dust let alone
well formed thoughts, so I ask you,


Why does it matter?

It doesn't.
Not one word, not one syllable
of my opinion makes a difference

Gimme my crown,
I'm the queen of nowhere;
Knower of fuck all, the invisible woman,

so again, I ask, why does it matter?

Aren't there a billion others about
that could tell you what you need to hear?

The world is full of Pubic Opinion Judges
that could certainly fulfil your desire
for unfettered truth.

They, whose minds turn
as long as their mouths are open?
Surely they are better suited to your
requirements

than some transparent fool who believes that
she's human.

MELANIE MCCURDIE

## *The Lanta Motel*

She didn't expect me
Not really, deep in her heart
She was sure she'd been fooling herself
That I'd played along, one last trick
I could smell the hope in the air on the other
side
Hear the sharp intake of breath
When I knocked on the door of room 147
At the Lanta Motel on highway 8

I'll never forget her expression
Lustful and fearful at once
When I swept her into my arms
And had her there
on the floor
in every way possible
Loving how she fought,
lamely at first
Then harder as I went deeper

When she came alive, scratching
Clawing my face and neck
The marks burned as I dug my thumbs
into the soft sides of her throat

Feeling her shake beneath me

Her trickling stream a river
And her eyes full of my image
I shot my load into her
It felt like it would never stop

Letting go of her neck,
I slammed into her one more time
Expecting at least a squeak or a moan
But she only stared, slack-jawed and glazed
At the door, perhaps for Salvation
Finding only me

Now she is food for the fishes
In the ocean below
By this time tomorrow
I'll be in a new town, who knows
Maybe your town
And maybe my next girlfriend
Will be you

MELANIE MCCURDIE

## *Smoking Gun*

Just *I Love You* and

**BANG**

You're dead and you fall to the floor
My painted fingertips are shaking.

The smoking gun in my hand is
pointed at the door
And I watch your hands jitter a weak vibrato
on the on the floor

The fists pounding on the door rattle the frame
The heels of your boots keeping time on the
floor
There's a shadow on the door
And footsteps grinding on the floor

You lay cooling on the floor
Many shadows in the glass on the door

And your blood drains onto the floor
Voices whispering leak under the door

I sit astride you on the floor
And take another aim at the door

## Déjà Vu

She can't shake the feeling of déjà vu that keeps sweeping over her, that itching cold finger tracing her spine as she shivers in the heat of the bonfire that had been stoked to a fury.

There, he's going to trip over a root and fall on his face. She's going to lean over and kiss that really cute guy sitting across from her as he continues to stare at the bad boy across the way, she thinks. watching it play out before her eyes. Does that mean he is here too?

She sweeps her eyes across the crowd of people, looking for the man who had plagued her dreams for months, so much so that sleep was something she keeps looking forward to. Craving.

Nowhere to be seen, and she lets the breath she'd been holding loose, releasing the burn that was aching there. The sound is in relief and more than a little disappointment.

It isn't sleep she craves, its *him*. She desires his touch like the ocean craves the sandy shore; her dreams are so real that she wakes with marks on her skin and often in mid orgasm.

Her eyes fall upon a man in the shadows, his eyes are glittering in the firelight and he wears a smile that made her squirm with fear and delight. At last, He is here.

## Spun Sugar

Your name tastes like spun sugar on my tongue, she said with a smile that lit up her eyes. The fireworks behind her made her glow and my heart nearly exploded with joy. Until then, my whole world was a circus and I the silly fool who stuck his head in the lion's mouth night after night.

But then, she stood on her tiptoes and whispered my name. closing her eyes with her lips curved and upturned, waiting and I wanted to. I wanted to kiss the corner of her smile and did. She melted against me, sweet as maple candy, touching me wherever she could reach. *Tracing your image with my hands, in my mind.* She sighed into my ear when I laughed.

She burned like a candle, in my arms and even the cobwebbed corners of her soul seemed illuminated as I laid her down on the old bear rug. We drank glass up9on glass of the dark red wine that tasted like oak barrels and summer cherries and when she laughed with her head thrown back in gleeful giggles,

I jumped to my feet and pulled her to me.and laid her down in front of the fire on that old bear rug; I laid her down and loved her, covered her in kisses.

My lips memorized each curve and edge as she chanted her pleasure against my shoulder, her small even teeth leaving impressions on my skin. When she exploded, she kissed me as she smoldered, my own pleasure lit her from the inside and she shivered.  Spun Sugar. she whispered then groaned, my name sweeter than chocolate and twice as rich.

She called me Spun Sugar from that night on, whenever the lights were low and the firebugs crackled. Everything was right with the world in her arms, even the way she would laugh as she stared in my eyes and prickled my heart with her wide-eyed delight.

Consummating our love once was like the first time, every time and the linking our bodies with open mouthed gazes was decadence beyond belief.  My hands, they squeezed her firm ripe breasts and then her throat as she struggled towards ecstasy and I rode the wave of her fight.

Fading roses, we were frozen together with her inner muscles grasping and releasing along with the fluttery caresses of her fingertips on my cheeks. Her heartbeat was so strong that her nipples quivered and her back arched hard against my body.

I could feel her battle to complete our loving act but I didn't let go of her throat.

Looking back now, I can see that I loved her to death. Those moments that seem so insignificant, they stay with you forever.

MELANIE MCCURDIE

## *Once Upon a Time*

Once upon a time,
in a land gone from mind,
in a secret grove of ancient trees,
there lived a woman.

Just a woman, you say?

Indeed, just a woman, of flesh and bone,
not unlike any other,
and different all the same.

Inside her lay a knowledge,
an untapped magic that danced
in her footsteps and sparkled the
fathomless pits that were her eyes.

She moved about her humble dwelling,
drifting here and there,
her mouth a grim line, where once it smiled
to charm everyone it fell upon.

She paused to sigh,
to glance out the window, with
it's wide thrown shutters affording her
the glorious view of the star soaked sky.

The twinkling like his eyes,
diamonds on velvet.
Another long exhale of air,
a sorrowful sound and she stepped from the
warmth of her home, over the threshold and
into Nature's chilly embrace,
where she shivered delicately
in her memories

Above, the Heavens shone like a giant jewel,
a crackling rainbow too bright to see and
she felt it tremble in her teeth,
forcing her to shield her eyes against it.

A voice.
It sang a familiar refrain
that shivered her skin as though caressed
with unseen hand, and it awakened the
forgotten heat in her loins with a vengeance.

Come,
it urged melodically.
Lifting her slender hand to her lips,
she gasped, the beasts and monsters
that roamed nearby lost in her fear.

It cajoled, that voice, coaxing with its
lugubrious tones, *come, Lovely, dance.*

Slowly she lowered her hand,
trailing it over her dry lips
to her moist throat,
her breath coming in small sips.
Afraid, she appeared
But looks can be deceiving

The tune not a voice but a
trilling whistle growing ever closer,
ever more sinister,
for it seemed to mock the quick beating
of her rapidly throbbing heart

Silence greets her ears, heavy and
full of eyes, eyes on her, eyes with claws,
tearing at her dress.

*Closer -*

It enticed, that voice,
deep and full of insinuation.

Her smoldering desire became
a roaring hellbeast as she stepped
from safety to danger,
reached out her hand to darkness

And vanished

## ABOUT THE AUTHOR

I am a Canadian based writer who resides in Calgary, Alberta and am a Warrior Mom blessed with two challenging boys, Sam 14 and Davey 10. I am a rabid supporter of Independent Film and Publications, and a horror junkie with a taste for words, and bloodsauce. Most recently, I was voice talent to The Carmen Theatre Group as Maria Sanchez and I can be seen in The Orphan Killer 2: Bound x Blood, written and created by Matt Farnsworth.

Made in the USA
Lexington, KY
21 May 2019